THE CENTRE OF INDIAN CULTURE

THE CENTRE OF INDIAN CULTURE

RABINDRANATH TAGORE

GYAN

Published by

GYAN

Gyan Publishing House
5, Ansari Road
Daryaganj, New Delhi-110002
Phone: 011-47034999, 9811692060
E-mail: books@gyanbooks.com

Distribution Network
gyanbooks.com
India, USA, Canada, UK, Australia

ISBN: 978-93-6920-048-1 (HB)

First Published, 1919

2nd Impression 2025

Printed at: Gyan Press, Delhi.

THE CENTRE OF INDIAN CULTURE
Author: RABINDRANATH TAGORE

THE CENTRE OF INDIAN CULTURE

RABINDRANATH TAGORE

VISVA-BHARATI BOOKSHOP
2, COLLEGE SQUARE, CALCUTTA

THE CENTRE OF INDIAN CULTURE

THE question which I intend to discuss in the present paper is, what should be the ideal of education in India.

Instead of holding my listeners' minds in suspense till the very end, let me briefly give the answer in the beginning before entering into a detailed discussion. On each race is the duty laid to keep alight its own lamp of mind as its part in the illumination of the world. To break the lamp of any people is to deprive it of its rightful place in the world festival. He who has no light is unfortunate enough, but utterly miserable is he who, having it, has been deprived of it, or has forgotten all about it.

India has proved that it has its own mind, which has deeply thought and felt and tried to solve according to its light the problems of existence. The education of India is to enable this *mind* of India to find out truth, to make this truth its own wherever found and to give expression to it in such a manner as only it can do.

In order to carry this out, first of all the mind of India has to be concentrated and made conscious of itself and then only can it accept education from its teachers in a right spirit, judge it by its own standard and make use of it by its own creative power. The fingers must be joined together to take, as well as to give. So when we can bring the scattered minds of India into co-ordinated activity, they will then become receptive as well as creative

—and the waters of life will cease to slip through the gaps, to make sodden the ground beneath.

The next point is that, in education, the most important factor must be the inspiring atmosphere of creative activity. And therefore the primary function of our University should be the constructive work of knowledge. Men should be brought together and full scope given to them for their work of intellectual exploration and creation; and the teaching should be like the overflow water of this spring of culture, spontaneous and inevitable. Education can only become natural and wholesome when it is the direct fruit of a living and growing knowledge.

The last point is that our education should be in full touch with our complete life, economical, intellectual, æsthetic, social and spiritual; and our educational institutions should be in the very heart of our society, connected with it by the living bonds of varied co-operations. For true education is to realize at every step how our training and knowledge have organic connection with our surroundings.

II

All over India, there is a vague feeling of discontent in the air about our prevalent system of education. Signs have lately been numerous of a desire for a change—there seems to be an urgence of life in the subsoil of our national mind, sending forth new institutions and giving rise to new experiments. But it often happens that, because man's wish is so immediate to him, and so strong, it becomes difficult accurately to locate the exact exciting cause, to make sure of the object towards which it aspires.

The mind of our educated community has been brought up within the enclosure of the modern Indian educational system. It has grown as familiar to us as our own physical body, unconsciously giving rise in our mind to the belief that it can never be changed. Our imagination dare not soar beyond its limits; we are unable to see it and judge it from outside. We neither have the courage nor the heart to say that it has to be replaced by something else, because our own intellectual life has been its special product, for which we have a natural partiality and admiration.

And yet there lurks, in some depth of our self-satisfaction, a thorn, which does not let us sleep in comfort. When the secret pricking goes on for some time, we, in our fretfulness, try to ascribe the cause of our irritation to some outside intrusion. We say that the only thing wrong in our education is that it is not in our absolute control; that the boat is sea-worthy, only the helm has to be in our own hands to save it from wreckage. Lately, most of our attempts to establish national schools and universities were made with the idea that it was external independence which was needed. We forget that the same weakness in our character, or in our circumstances, which inevitably draws us on to the slippery slope of imitation, will pursue us when our independence is merely of the outside. For then our freedom will become the freedom to imitate the foreign institutions, thus bringing our evil fortune under the influence of the conjunction of two malignant planets—those of imitation and the badness of imitation—producing a machine-made University, which is made with a bad machine.

As it often happens with the party which has been beaten in a game for the partners of the same side to ascribe the failure to one another's stupidity, so, in our discredited system of education, we two partners—our foreign authorities and ourselves—are following the same course of mutual recrimination. It is very likely that the blame can be justly apportioned between both of us; yet I always think it is more a matter of academic interest than anything else to wrangle with the other fellow about his share of the futility when we ourselves were also deeply involved. What is of real practical importance is for us to know what was our own contribution to the deficiency we complain of.

Those who feel pity for the Sudras may say that only the Brahmins were responsible for placing the former in a degraded condition. But, without discussing the merit of such an assertion, it has to be admitted that it would be of real benefit to the Sudras to be told that it was they who were responsible for weakly allowing the helpless Brahmins to humiliate them.

So let us forget the other party in this concern. Let us blame our own weakness in being obsessed with the idea that we must have some artificial wooden legs of an education of foreign-make simply because we imagine that we have no legs of our own to stand upon. I have heard of a similar case of an unfortunate man who got drowned in shallow water because he imagined that he had gone out of his depth.

The mischief is that as soon as the idea of a University enters our mind, the idea of a Cambridge University, Oxford University, and a host of other European Universities, rushes in at the same time and fills the whole space. We then imagine that our salvation lies in a selection of the best points of each patched together in an eclectic perfection. We forget that the European Universities are living organic parts of the life of Europe, where each found its natural birth. Patching up noses, and other small missing fractions of our features, with skins from foreign limbs is allowed in modern surgery; but to build up a whole man by piecing together foreign fragments is beyond the resources of science, not only for the present time, but let us fervently hope, for all time to come.

The European University comes before our vision, full-grown. That is why we cannot think of a University except as a fully developed institution. The sight of my neighbour, with a sturdy son to help and support him, may naturally provoke in my mind an envious wish to have a son myself. But if my wish be to have a full-grown son all at once, then, in my hurry, I may stumble upon somebody who is fully grown up, but who is no son to me at all. An impatient craving for results and an unfortunate weakness for imitation have led us to cherish just such an unnatural desire for a National University, full-fledged from its very birth. So that most of our endeavours become fruitless, or else the only fruit they produce is of the class of lacquer-ware fruit, which may rival the real thing in size and shape and colouring, but which one has to beware of biting, much more of taking into the stomach. These solidly complete Universities, over which our country is brooding, are like hard-boiled eggs from which you cannot expect chickens to come out.

Not only ourselves, but our European school-master himself seems to have forgotten that his University has grown with the growth of the nation he belongs to, and that its material magnificence was not in its beginning and does not belong to its essential truth. No doubt the time has come when he can comfortably afford to forget, in his own case, that it was the indigent monks who were the source of his educational proficiency in the first instance, and that most of the students at one time were poor. But when he affects to ignore the fact that, in a poor country like India, the material features of our University must not assume more importance than we can bear, when he cruelly forgets that the insufficiency of our schools and colleges must not be made still narrower in scope by cutting down space and increasing furniture, then it becomes disastrous for our people.

I quite understand that food and the utensils to eat it out of are both needful to man. But where there is a shortage of food, a parsimony in regard to utensils also becomes necessary. To make the paraphernalia of our Education so expensive that Education itself becomes difficult of attainment would be like squandering all one's money in buying money-bags.

We in the East have had to arrive at our own solution of the problem of life. We have, as far as possible, made our food and clothing unburdensome; and this our very climate has taught us to do. We require openings in the walls more than the walls themselves. Light and air have more to do with our wearing apparel than the weavers' loom. The sun makes for us the heat-producing factors which elsewhere are required from food-stuffs. All these natural advantages have moulded our life to a particular shape, which I cannot believe it will be profitable to ignore in the case of our education.

I do not seek to glorify poverty. But simplicity is of greater price than the appendages of luxury. The simplicity of which I speak is not merely the effect of a lack of superfluity; it is one of the signs of perfection. When this dawns on mankind, the unhealthy fog which now besmirches civilization will be lifted. It is for lack of this simplicity that the necessaries of life have become so rare and costly.

Most things in the civilized world, such as eating and merry-making, education and culture, administration and litigation, occupy more than their legitimate space. Much of their burden is needless; and in bearing it civilized man may be showing great strength, but little skill. To the gods, viewing this from on high, it must seem like the flounderings of a giant who has got out of his depth and knows not how to swim; who, as he keeps muddying the whole pool by his needlessly powerful efforts, cannot get rid of the idea that there must be some virtue in this display of strength.

When the simplicity of fulness awakens in the West, then work, enjoyment, and education alike, will find their true strength in becoming easy. When this will happen I have no idea, but till then we must, with bowed heads, continue to listen to lectures telling us that the highest education is to be had only in the tallest edifices.

To the extent that forms and appendages are the outgrowth of the soul, to ignore them is to be impoverished—this I know. But though Europe has been trying, she has not yet discovered the golden mean. Why, then, should obstacles be placed in the way of our attempting to find it out for ourselves? To be simple without becoming poorer is the problem which each must solve according to his temperament. But while we are ever ready to accept the subject-matter of education from outside, it is too bad to thrust on us the temperament as well.

This attitude of our teacher has affected the minds of his disciple and in our pursuit of magnitude we are becoming careless of reality.

III

When the National Council of Education was being founded in Bengal, I asked one of its enthusiastic workers whether he really believed that the great spreading tree of a University could come into being, with root and branch and foliage all complete, in a day. His reply was that if not, it would not succeed in capturing the imagination of the country; so that the complete thing must be held forth from the beginning. Well, it was duly held forth, the imagination of the country was captured, money flowed in, and nothing seemed to be wanting except just one casual factor—the truth—the truth which never disdains small beginnings, which is never ashamed to carry its immense future in a tiny frail package. And the imitation tree, after vainly trying to prove its fruitfulness, has shrunk and shrivelled to such fragile precariousness that it does not have material enough to deceive even itself. So let us repeat, it does not follow that by merely founding a University oneself, and keeping it under one's own control, it can be made one's own.

Let us, then, try to find out what is the hidden cause of dissatisfaction that is troubling our minds. The fact is, it was nearly a hundred years ago when we first entered our English school, and we have not even yet been able to get out of it; we have permanently remained school-boys. We have got the same kind of shelter in it as the mouse in the trap—it threatens to be so awkwardly everlasting.

No one has been able to give us a complete definition of life, because, at every moment, it transcends its parts and is mysteriously more than what we get from its analysis. What it gives out is far greater, in quality and value, than the materials it consumes. It is not a mere sum total of the carbon, nitrogen, and other ingredients which it takes in with its food. Our mind, also, in the fulness of its life, is infinitely greater than the information it appropriates, the training it acquires. That education is true, which acknowledges the mind to be a living thing, and therefore stimulates it to give out more in quality and quantity than is imparted to it from outside. And we are to judge our education by this standard.

Therefore the question is, whether, in our intellectual

career in the modern time, we have given more than we have received, and created something which is our own. For when any race of men becomes a mere burden on the world, rendering no satisfactory account of the cost it imposes upon society, this, for it, is worse than death. For this is the intolerably mean situation of remaining under the charge of perpetual misappropriation.

As for us, far from having given our University more than we received, we have not even rendered back full measure. We have been repeating great words, learning great truths, looking on great examples, but in return we have simply become clerks, deputy magistrates, pleaders, or physicians.

Not that it is a small thing to be, for instance, a physician. But though our physicians are now practising in every town and village and hamlet of the country, and though many of them are of good repute and making money, all this extensive experience of theirs has not resulted in any new theory, or great fact, being added to the science of medicine. Like good school-boys, they have only applied with over-cautious precision just what they have learnt. And who shall make good the vital thing that is lost when students never become masters?

Yet I cannot admit that this is due to any inherent defect in our natural powers. There was a long period in the past, during which the science of healing with us was a living growth, spreading its different off-shoots and branches all over our country. That teaches us at least this much that in those days our mind was in living connection with its acquirements ; that then, we did not merely learn by rote, but made our own observations and experiments; that we tried to discover principles and build hypotheses and apply them to life.

Where has this initiative and courage of ours departed? Why do we tread so carefully, so fearfully, under the load of our learning? Is it because we were born to be serfs, permanently bending under the burden of another's intellectual acquisitions? Never!

For even in spite of the scarceness of opportunities and narrowness of prospects, in spite of our present defective education, which has been starved of all life elements, a few great men of science like Jagadischandra and Praphullachandra, and a great scholar and thinker like Brajendranath, have made their appearance in our country, proving that the power of true originality is not lacking among our people, only it is trampled down under the dead pressure of a mechanical method and the callousness of contemptuous discouragement.

IV

All organic beings live like a flame, a long way beyond themselves. They have thus a smaller and a larger body. The former is visible to the eye; it can be touched, captured and bound. The latter is indefinite; it has no fixed boundaries, but is widespread both in space and time. When we see a foreign University, we see only its smaller body—its buildings, its furniture, its regulations, its syllabus; its larger body is not present to us. But as the kernel of the cocoanut is in the whole cocoanut, so the University, in the case of Europeans, is in their society, in their parliament, in their literature, in the numerous activities of their corporate life. They have their thoughts published in their books, as well as the living men who think those thoughts and criticize, compare and disseminate them. One common medium of mind connects their teachers and students in an educational relationship which is living and luminous. In short their education has its permanent vessel which is their own mind; its permanent supply which is their own living spring of culture; its permanent field for irrigation which is their own social life. This organic unity of their mind and life and culture has enabled them to seek truth from all lands and all times, and to make it vitally one with their own culture which is the basis of their civilization.

On the other hand, those who, like our present Indian students, have to rely upon books, not truly for their mental sustenance, but for some external advantage, are sure to become anæmic in their intellects, like babies solely fed with artificial food. They never have intellectual courage, because they never see the process and the environment of those thoughts which they are compelled to learn—and thus they lose the historical sense of all ideas, never knowing the perspective of their growth. They are hypnotized by the sharp black and white of the printed words, formed and fixed, which hide their human genesis. They not only borrow a foreign culture, but also a foreign standard of judgment; and thus, not only is the money not theirs, but not even the pocket. Their education is a chariot that does not carry them in it, but drags them behind it. The sight is pitiful and very often comic. The modern European culture, whose truth and strength lie in its fluid mobility, comes to us rigidly fixed, almost like our own *Sastras*, about which our minds have to remain passively uncritical because of their supposed divine origin.

This has made us miss the dynamic character of living truth. The English mind from the Early Victorian to the mid-Victorian, and from the mid-Victorian to the post-Victorian period of its growth, has been passing through different moods and standards. But we, who take our lessons from the English, can only accept some one or other of these moods and standards as fixed; we cannot naturally move with the moving mind of our teacher, but only hop from one point to another and miss the modulation of life. We securely confine all our intellectual faith, either within the utilitarianism of Bentham and Mill, or the spiritualism of Carlyle and Ruskin, or the paradoxicalism, startling lazy minds into truth, in which Chesterton and Bernard Shaw excel; and we fail to notice their relation of inevitable action and reaction. We boast of the up-to-dateness of our education; we forget that the mission of all education is to lead us beyond the present date.

V

Communication of life can only be through a living agency. And culture, which is the life of mind, can only be imparted through man to man. Book learning, or scriptural texts, may merely make us pedants. They are static and quantitative; they accumulate and are hoarded up under strict guards. Culture grows and moves and multiplies itself in life.

The students of the European Universities not only have their human environment of culture in their society, they also acquire their learning direct from their teachers. They have their sun to give them light; it is the sun of the human relationship between the teachers and the students. We have our hard flints, which give us disconnected sparks after toilsome blows; and the noise is a great deal more than the light. These flints are the abstractions of learning; they are solid methods, inflexible and cold.

To our misfortune we have, in our own country, all the furniture of the European University—except the human teacher. We have, instead, merely purveyors of book-lore, in whom the paper god of the bookshop seems to have made himself vocal. And, as a natural result, we find our students to be 'untouchable', even to our Indian professors. These teachers distribute their doles of mental food, gingerly and from a dignified distance, raising walls of notebooks between themselves and their students. This kind of food is neither relished, nor does it give nourishment. It is a famine ration strictly regulated, to save us, not from emaciation, but only from absolute death. It holds out no hope of that culture which is far in excess of man's mere necessity; it is certainly less than enough, and far less than a feast.

Until we are in a position to prove that the world has need of us and cannot afford to do without us, that we are not merely hangers-on of the world-culture—beggars who cannot repay—so long must our sole hope lie in gaining others' favours. And these we must extort, sometimes by lamentations, sometimes by flattery, sometimes by menial service, and show other constitutional methods of wagging tails.

No one will feel any anxiety to minister to us, to save us, if we have nothing to offer worthy of being reverently accepted. But whom are we to blame? Where is there space enough, lying fallow on this earth, for men who merely live and do not produce? How can they build an infirmary as big as the country itself? The hard fact must be laid to heart that we shall never get anything even if it be given to us. For it is only the lake, and not the desert, which can accept and retain a contribution from the heaven's cloud because, in its depth, the receiving and the giving have become one. Only to him who hath is given, otherwise the gift is insulted and he, also, who receives it.

But we have been so used to living on beggars' doles that we cannot bring ourselves really to believe in this truth. We are always afraid lest we should lose some petty advantage in our attempts to acquire true learning, lest our preparedness for clerical work should be delayed, lest the English of our petition-writing lose its correct grammatical whine. Our education to us is like the carriage to a horse; a bondage, the dragging of which merely serves to provide it with food and shelter in the stable of its master; the horse has not the same freedom of relationship with the carriage as its owner, and therefore the carriage ever remains for it an imposition of beggarly necessity.

VI

Let me here quote a precedent to show how a University can work, which has been born and has grown on national soil, and how with a different history futility comes about.

In that age of Europe which is called dark, when the lamp of Rome went out at the onslaught of the barbarians, Ireland, amongst all countries of the West, was the land where culture reared its head. Students from other parts of Europe used to flock there for education. They used to get their board, lodging and books free—something like our own Sanskrit *pathasalas*. The Irish monks revived the flame of the smouldering torch of Christian religion and culture all over Europe. Charlemagne took the help of Clemens, a learned Irishman, in founding the University of Paris. There are many other proofs of the height to which Irish culture had attained. Though its origin was in Rome, yet through a long period of segregation it became imbued with the life and mind of the people and acquired a genius which was characteristically Irish. And this culture had for its medium the Irish language.

When the Danes and the English invaded Ireland, they set fire to the Irish colleges, destroyed their libraries, and killed or scattered the monks and students. Nevertheless, in those parts of the country, which still remained independent and free from these outrages, the work of education continued to be carried on in the mother-tongue, till, in the time of Queen Elizabeth, Ireland was wholly conquered and finally lost its indigenous Universities. Thereafter, being deprived of the atmosphere of culture and study, the Irish language fell into contempt, as fit only for the lower classes. Then, in the nineteenth century, the National School movement was set afoot, and the Irish, with their ingrained love of learning, welcomed it with uncritical enthusiasm.

The idea of the so-called national schools was to mould the Irish on the Anglo-Saxon pattern. But, whether for good or for evil, Providence has fashioned each race on such different lines that to put one into the coat of another results in a misfit. When the National School movement was started, eighty per cent of Irishmen were using their own language. But the Irish boys, under pain of many penalties, were made to give up their own language altogether, and the ban was also extended to the study of their own history.

The result was just what might be expected. Mental numbness spread all over the country. Irish-speaking boys, who entered the schools with their intelligence and curiosity alive, left them mental cripples, with a distaste for all study. The reason was simple. The method was machine-like, the result parrot-like.

The conditions in one country are never quite the same as those in another. Britain's educational policy in Ireland may not exactly resemble her policy in India. But there is at least one vital point of similarity in regard to the result—our mind is not in our studies. In fact, it has been wholly ignored that we have a mind of our own. That is to say, the engineering feat of skill in digging the canal, with its numerous locks and *bunds*, has been marvellous, and the cost considerable—only the water refuses to flow through. The engineers condemn the water for its obstreperousness; we take the side of the water and condemn the engineers. In the meanwhile, the great gaping gulf remains arid. Let me say, in a whisper, behind the backs of these irate engineers, that the natural drainage of the country has been tampered with and the country is taking its revenge.

VII

For the perfect irrigation of learning, a foreign language cannot be a true medium. This is a truism, whose utterance would bore men to sleep, or to something worse, in any other part of the world; but in our country truisms appear as dangerous heresies, rousing our phlegmatic souls into active hostility. Therefore, for us, all truisms are a tonic, though we relish platitudes far better. And this makes me bold to reiterate that when we are compelled to learn through the medium of English, the knocking at the gate and turning of the key take away the best part of our life. The feast may be waiting for us inside the room, but the difficulty and delay of admission spoil our appetite and the long privation permanently injures our stomach. The ideas are very late in coming to us, and the tediously long trial of our teeth over the grinding of the grammar, and a system of spelling, which is devoid of all conscience, takes away our relish for the food when it does come at last.

If you want to grow a tree on the sandy soil of a rainless desert, then you not only have to borrow your seed from some distant land, but also the soil itself and the water. Yet, after the immense trouble you have taken, the tree grows up miserably stunted; and even if it does bear fruit, the seeds do not mature. The education which we receive from our universities takes it for granted that it is for cultivating a hopeless desert, and that not only the mental outlook and the knowledge, but also the whole language must bodily be imported from across the sea. And this makes our education so nebulously distant and unreal, so detached from all our associations of life, so terribly costly to us in time, health and means, and yet so meagre of results.

So far as my own experience of teaching goes, a considerable proportion of pupils are naturally deficient in the power of learning languages. Such may find it barely possible to matriculate with an insufficient understanding of the English language, while in the higher stages disaster is inevitable. There are, moreover, other reasons why English cannot be mastered by a large majority of Indian boys. First of all, to accommodate this language in their minds, whose ingrained habit has been to think in an Eastern tongue, is as much a feat as fitting an English sword into the scabbard of a scimitar. Then again, very few boys have the means of getting anything like a proper grounding in English at the hands of a competent teacher—the sons of the poor certainly have not.

So, like the Hanuman of our ancient Epic, who, not knowing which herb might be wanted, had to carry away the whole mountain top, these boys, unable to use the language intelligently, have to carry in their heads the whole of the book by rote. Those who have extraordinary memories may thus manage to carry on to the end, but this cannot be expected of the poor fellows with only average brain power.

The point is—is the crime committed by this large number of boys, who, owing to congenital or accidental causes, have been unable to become proficient in the English language, so heinous that they must be sentenced to perpetual exile by the University? In England at one time thieves used to get hanged. But this penal code is even harsher, because the extreme penalty is imposed for *not* being able to cheat! For if it be cheating to take a book into the examination hall hidden in one's clothes, why not when the whole of its contents is smuggled in within the head?

However, I do not wish to lay any charge against those fortunate crammers who manage to get across. But those who are left behind, to whom the Hooghly Bridge is closed, may they not have some kind of ferry, if not a steam launch, at least a country boat? What a terrible waste of national material to cut off all higher educational facilities from the thousands of pupils who have no gift for acquiring a foreign tongue, but who possess the intellect and desire to learn.

I know what the counter-argument will be. Men will say: "You want to give higher education in the vernaculars, but what about the text books?" I am aware that there are none. But unless higher education is given in the vernacular languages, how are text books to come into existence? We cannot very well expect a mint to go on working if the coins are refused circulation.

VIII

Another lesson to be learnt from the Irish example is that, in the natural course of things, the water comes first and then comes the fish—it is the presence of the learned men which draws the students round them, if their wish is to learn, and not merely to be branded, like a saleable commodity, with the stamp of their market-value.

In an age of great mental vitality, when men were there whose minds overflowed with thoughts and learning, the culture centres of Nalanda and Taxila were naturally formed in India. But, because we have been accustomed merely to branding institutions while receiving our education, therefore even in our attempts at founding national universities we begin from the wrong end—the students come first in our mind, and then we cast about for the teachers. It is like the vagary of an absent-minded Creator who takes great pains in creating a tail and then suddenly finds that the head is missing. We seat our guests at the table, and afterwards discover that the cooking has not been commenced. So the sumptuousness has to be made evident in the menu to keep the imagination of the famished fully occupied—we have to shout with an exaggerated vehemence for the dishes which never come, and make up for the lack in the food supply with deafening noise.

When the best part of our anxiety goes to secure students, we are obliged to think of laying ground baits for the imagination of the country. All in a night, long syllabuses have to be got ready, the hatred of the foreigner stirred up, frantic appeals made to Mother India, and all kinds of hypnotic texts uttered, to distract and confound the minds of men.

For the sake of the sanity of our mind and reasonableness of our purpose, let us for once throw to the winds all anxiety as to syllabuses, and as to students also. Let us drive out of our thoughts the holy images of our existing educational institutions, on which we have steadfastly meditated so long.

And then let us pray that those, who have successfully passed through the discipline of cultivating their minds, who are ready to produce and therefore to impart, may deign to come together and take up their seats of studious striving, doing intently their own work of exploration and discovery in the region of knowledge. In this way will be concentrated the power which shall be adequate for the spontaneous creation of a University, from within ourselves, in all the truth of life.

We must know that this concentration of intellectual forces of the country is the most important mission of a University, for it is like the nucleus of a living cell, the centre of the creative life of the national mind.

IX

The bringing about of an intellectual unity in India is, I am told, difficult to the verge of impossibility owing to the fact that India has so many different languages.

But every people in the world, in order to attain its greatness, must solve some great problem for itself, or accept defeat and degradation. All true civilizations have been built upon the bedrock of difficulties. Those who have rivers for their water supply are to be envied, but those who have not must dig wells and find water from the difficult depth of their own soil. But let us never imagine that dust can be made to do the duty of the water simply because it is more easily available. We must bravely accept the inconvenient fact of the diversity of our languages, and at the same time know that a foreign language, like foreign soil, may be good for pot culture, but not for that cultivation which is widely and permanently necessary for the maintenance of life.

Then let us admit that India is not like any one of the great countries of Europe, which has its one language, but like Europe herself branching out into different peoples having different languages. And yet Europe has a common civilization with an intellectual unity which is not based upon uniformity of language.

In the earlier stage of her culture the whole of Europe had Latin for her language of learning. It was like her intellectual bud-time, when all her petals of self-expression were closed into one point. But the perfection of her mental unfolding was not represented by that oneness of her literary vehicle. When the great European countries found their individual languages, then only the true federation of cultures became possible in the West and the very differences of the channels made the commerce of ideas in Europe so richly copious and so variedly active. In fact, when natural differences find their harmony, then it is true unity; but artificial uniformity leads to lifelessness. We can well imagine what the loss to European civilization would be, if France, Italy, Germany, England, through their separate agencies, did not contribute to the common coffers their individual earnings. And we know why, when the German culture tried to assert its sole dominance, it was hailed as a calamity by all Europe.

There was a time with us when India also had her common language of culture in Sanskrit. But, for the completeness of her commerce of thought, she must have all her vernaculars attaining their perfect powers, through which her different peoples may manifest their differences of genius to the full. This can never be done through a language which is foreign, containing its own peculiar associations which are sure to hamper our freedom of thought and creation. The use of English inevitably tends to turn our mind for its source of inspiration towards the West, with which we can never be in close touch of life; and therefore our education will mostly remain sterile, or produce incongruities. The diversity of our languages should not be allowed to frighten us; but we should be warned of the futility of borrowing the language of our culture from a far-away land, making stagnant and shallow that which is fluid near its source.

It is unthinkable that we should cease to write petitions in English, or abdicate our seats in the obscure region of the subordinate service. For the present, we have sorrowfully to acknowledge the fact that, English being our court language, it acts like an artificial tariff, gradually driving away our mother-tongue from our life of culture into the insignificance of domestic use.

But this is perpetuating for us the heavy and costly burden of all the alien features of our Government, incomprehensible to the masses of our population. It involves the cruel necessity of a host of English-knowing middlemen for carrying on relationship with the governing power in matters of the smallest detail. I believe that India is the only country in the world where the Government has an Agricultural Department, which publishes its bulletins for the benefit of the cultivators in a language unknown to them, making these poor cultivators pay the cost of this heartless joke played upon themselves.

The Government has expensive arrangements made for everything necessary to be translated from the vernaculars into English, in order to make the administrative work of a foreign country lazily convenient for the few English officials engaged in this task. But, for the three hundred millions of people inhabiting this country, are kept strictly *purda-nashin*, behind a foreign language, the codes of law, the proceedings of the legislative councils, the lectures of the Governors addressed to the people, and all the important Government communications affecting their life. This makes us wonder all the more at the last remnant of the sense of humour exhibited in our railway stations, where the names are actually inscribed in the Indian alphabets to help the Indian travellers. In fact, our rulers have made their duties cheap for themselves, but immensely expensive for the people they have come to govern.

This has created a most unnatural situation for us, making our own language an obstacle in our pathway of success, thus generating among our educated men a humiliating pride in being able to perform the rope-dancer's feat of skill by leading their knowledge of English over the perilously thin line of correct grammar. And merely for this we have no other option but fondly to overlook all vital defects in our present system and with grateful tears accept from its hands a stone in place of bread. For not only have we to pay the cost of our government with taxes, but also with our own language and with our own true culture, upon which depends the salvation of our motherland for all time to come.

X

We must therefore think of the seat of our Indian learning as in excess of, and quite apart from, the existing university-controlled schools and colleges. Let these lumbering machines be relegated to a place among our law courts, our offices, our police stations, gaols, asylums, and other paraphernalia of civilization.

If our country wants fruit and shade, let it abandon brick-and-mortar erections and come down to the soil. Why cannot we boldly avow that we shall nurture our own life-force as naturally as the pupils who used to gather round the teachers in the forest retreats of the Vedic age ; or at Nalanda or Taxila during the Buddhist era ; or as they gather even now, in the day of our downfall, in our *tols* and *chatuspathis*?

We must beware even of calling it a University. For the name itself is bound to rouse an irrepressible tendency to comparison and feeble imitation. My suggestion is that we should generate somewhere a centripetal force, which will attract and group together from different parts of our land and different ages all our own materials of learning and thus create a complete and moving orb of Indian culture.

XI

A pupil of an Anglo-vernacular school in Allahabad was once asked to define a river. The clever little fellow gave a perfectly correct definition. When he was asked what river he had seen, this unfortunate mite, living at the confluence of the Ganges and Jumna, replied that he had not seen any. He dimly had an idea that his familiar world (which so easily came to him through the medium of his own direct consciousness) could never be the great learned world of geography. In later life, he must have got the information that even his own country had its place in geography and actually had its rivers. But suppose this news did not reach him at all, till some foreign traveller told him one day that his was a great big country, that the Himalayas were great big mountains, that the Indus, Ganges, Brahmaputra were great big rivers—the shock of it could not but upset his mental balance, and in the reaction against the self-contempt he had nursed so long, he would lose no time in making himself absurdly hoarse by shouting that other countries were merely countries, but his was heaven itself! His previous understanding of the world was wrong—due to his ignorance. His subsequent understanding of the world was worse—it was ludicrously false with the falsehood of sophisticated foolishness.

The same thing happens in the case of our Indian culture. Because of the want of opportunity in our course of study, we take it for granted that India had no culture, or next to none. Then, when we hear from foreign pundits some echo of the praises of India's culture, we can contain ourselves no longer and rend the sky with the shout that all other cultures are merely human, but ours is divine—a special creation of Brahmá! And this leads us to that moral dipsomania, which is the hankering after the continual stimulation of self-flattery.

We should remember that the doctrine of special creation is out of date, and the idea of a specially favoured race belongs to a barbaric age. We have come to understand in modern times that any special truth, or special culture, which is wholly dissociated from the universal, is not true at all. Only the prisoner condemned to a solitary cell is separate from the world. He who declares that India has been condemned by Providence to intellectual solitary confinement does not help to glorify her.

However that may be, if we are to create a centre of Indian culture, we must start with the belief that India has a culture, and one which is worthy of being imparted to all.

My mind feels a pull at its coat from the back at this point. I know a section of my countrymen are saying to me: "Not so fast. Let us know if you believe that our Indian culture is the best in the world, or, at least so good as to deserve a place of honour in our education."

Fortunately, in God's world, the tyranny of the one sole best is not tolerated. There are numerous varieties of the best to keep each other company. So let us not quarrel over that superlative adjective or take it too seriously.

It can be easily pointed out that our culture has its superstitions and its shortcomings. They show themselves too prominently only because its movement has stopped. European culture also has its superstitions. Its politics and its science are full of them. These do not become fatally unhealthy because they move and they change—just like their caste distinctions, which are not desperately oppressive because they are constantly moving.

Only a few years ago, Europe began to see the whole world through the mist of one scientific shibboleth, "the struggle for existence". This coloured her vision, and fixed her point of view. We, also, like a meekly obedient pupil, took the phrase from her and thought it a sign of imperfect education not to believe it. But already there is an indication of a change in this view, and facts are being brought to prove that the positive force which works at the basis of natural selection is the power of sympathy, the power to combine. In the nineteenth century, the message of political economy was unrestrained competition; in the twentieth, it is beginning to change into co-operation. This only proves that whatever hinders movement is bad.

There was a time when we in India worked at the problem of life; we freely made experiments; the solutions we arrived at then cannot be ignored merely because they are different from those of Europe. But they must move; they have to join the procession of man's discoveries; they must not lag behind and superciliously forget others, and be contemptuously forgotten themselves. We are to call them into line and to move to the drum-beat of life.

XII

Far too long have we kept our culture outcasted in the confines of our indigenous Sanskrit *pathasalas*—for undue respect makes for untouchability as much as undue contempt.

There was a time when the excess of dignity of the Mikado of Japan kept him practically a prisoner in his palace, with the result that not he, but the Shogun, was the real ruler. When it became necessary for him to reign in fact, he had to be brought forth from his seclusion into the public view. So was the culture of our Sanskrit *patha-sala* confined within itself, disdainfully ignoring all other cultures of the world. It was belauded, as having come straight from Brahmá's mouth, or Siva's matted locks, or some equally superhuman outlet of irruption, so that it was unlike anything else anywhere in the world, and had to be kept apart, guarded from contamination by the common people. Thus it became the Mikado of our country, while foreign culture, gaining strength from its perfect freedom of movement and growth and its humanness, dominated the situation like the Shogun. Our reverence is reserved for the one, but all our taxes are paid to the other. We may launch out invectives against the latter in private, we may lament over our slavery to it ; but, all the same, we sell our wife's ornaments and mortgage our ancestral home to pay its dues to the last farthing when we send our sons to its durbar.

It will not do to keep our culture so reverently shackled with chains of gold. The age has come when all artificial fences are breaking down. Only that will survive which is basically consistent with the universal ; while that which seeks safety in the out-of-the-way hole of the special will perish. The nursery of the infant should be secluded, its cradle safe. But the same seclusion, if continued after the infant has grown up, makes it weak in body and mind.

There was a time when China, Persia, Egypt, Greece and Rome had, each of them, to nurture its civilization in comparative seclusion. The greatness of the universal, however, which was more or less in each, grew strong within its protecting sheath of individuality. Now has come the age for co-ordination and co-operation. The seedlings, that were reared within their enclosures, must now be transplanted into the open fields. They must pass the test of the world-market, if their maximum value is to be obtained.

So we must prepare the grand field for the co-ordination of the cultures of the world, where each will give to and take from the other; where each will have to be studied through the growth of its stages in history. This adjustment of knowledge through comparative study, this progress in intellectual co-operation, is to be the key-note of the coming age. We may hug our holy aloofness from some imagined security of a corner, but the world will prove stronger than our corner, and it is our corner which will have to give way, receding and pressing against its walls till they burst on all sides.

But before we are in a position to stand a comparison with the other cultures of the world, or truly to co-operate with them, we must base our own structure on a synthesis of all the different cultures we have. When, taking our stand at such a centre, we turn towards the West, our gaze shall no longer be timid and dazed; our heads shall remain erect, safe from insult. For then we shall be able to take our own views of Truth, from the standpoint of our own vantage ground, thus opening out a new vista of thought before the grateful world.

XIII

All great countries have their vital centres for intellectual life, where a high standard of learning is maintained, where the minds of the people are naturally attracted to find their genial atmosphere, to prove their worth, to contribute their share to the country's culture, and thus to kindle on some common altar of the land a great sacrificial fire of intellect which may radiate the sacred light in all directions.

Athens was such a centre in Greece, Rome in Italy, and Paris is such to-day in France. Benares has been and still continues to be the centre of our Sanskrit culture. But Sanskrit learning does not exhaust all the elements of culture that exist in the present-day India.

If we take for granted what some people maintain, that European culture is the only one worth the name in our modern age, then the question comes to our mind: has it any natural centre in India? Has it any vital ever-flowing connection with her life? The answer is that not only has it none, but it never can have any; for the perennial centre of European culture is sure to be in Europe. And therefore, if we must accept it as the only source of light for our mind, then it would be like depending upon some star for our daybreak, which is the sun of a far distant alien sphere. The star may give us light, but not the day; it may give us direction in our voyage of exploration, but it can never open the full view of truth before our eyes. In fact, we can never use this star light for stirring sap in our invisible depths and giving colour and bloom to our life.

This is the reason why European education has become for India mere school lessons and no culture, a box of matches good for various uses, but not the morning in which the use and the beauty and all the subtle mysteries of life have blended in one.

And this is why the inner spirit of India is calling to us to establish in this land great centres, where all her intellectual forces will gather for the purpose of creation, and all her resources of knowledge and thought, Eastern and Western, will unite in perfect harmony. She is seeking for herself her modern Brahmavarta, her Mithila, of Janaka's time, her Ujjaini, of the time of Vikramaditya. She is seeking for the glorious opportunity when she will know her mind, and give her mind to the world, to help it in its progress; when she will be released from the chaos of scattered powers and the inertness of borrowed acquisition.

XIV

Let me state clearly that I have no distrust of any culture because of its foreign character. On the contrary, I believe that the shock of such forces is necessary for the vitality of our intellectual nature. It is admitted that much of the spirit of Christianity runs counter, not only to the classical culture of Europe, but to the European temperament altogether. And yet this alien movement of idea, constantly running against the natural mental current of Europe, has been the most important factor in strengthening and enriching her civilization on account of the very antagonism of its direction. In fact, the European vernaculars first woke up to life and fruitful vigour owing to the impact of this foreign thought power with all its oriental forms and feelings. The same thing is happening in India. The European culture has come to us not only with its knowledge but with its velocity. Though our assimilation of it is imperfect and the consequent aberrations numerous, still it is rousing our intellectual life from its inertia of formal habits into glowing consciousness by the very contradiction it offers to our own mental traditions.

What I object to is the artificial arrangement by which this foreign education tends to occupy all the space of our national mind and thus kills, or hampers, the great opportunity for the creation of a new thought power by a new combination of truths. It is this which makes me urge that all the elements in our own culture have to be strengthened, not to resist the Western culture, but truly to accept and assimilate it, and use it for our food and not as our burden; to get mastery over this culture, and not to live at its outskirts as the hewers of texts and drawers of book-learning.

XV

The main river of Indian culture has flowed in four streams—the Vedic, the Puranic, the Buddhist, and the Jain. It had its source in the heights of the Indian consciousness.

But a river belonging to a country is not fed by its own waters alone. The Tibetan Bramhaputra is a tributary to the Indian Ganges. Contributions have similarly found their way to India's original culture. The Muhammadan, for example, has repeatedly come into India from outside, laden with his own stores of knowledge and feeling and his wonderful religious democracy, bringing freshet after freshet to swell the current. In our music, our architecture, our pictorial art, our literature, the Muhammadans have made their permanent and precious contribution. Those who have studied the lives and writings of our medieval saints, and all the great religious movements that sprang up in the time of the Muhammadan rule, know how deep is our debt to this foreign current that has so intimately mingled with our life.

And then has descended upon us the later flood of Western culture, which bids fair to break through all banks and bounds, merging all the other streams in its impetuous rush. If we can but make a separate course, through which this last may flow, we shall be saved from an irruption, whose cost may one day prove out of all proportion to its contribution, however large.

So, in our centre of Indian learning, we must provide for the co-ordinated study of all these different cultures—the Vedic, the Puranic, the Buddhist, the Jain, the Islamic, the Sikh, and the Zoroastrian. And side by side with them the European—for only then shall we be able to assimilate the last. A river flowing within banks is truly our own, but our relations with a flood are disastrously the opposite.

It is needless to add that, along with those languages in which lies stored our ancestral wealth of wisdom, we must make room for the study of all our great vernaculars which carry the living stream of the mind of modern India. Along with this study of our living languages, we must include our folk literature, in order truly to know the psychology of our people and the direction towards which our underground current of life is moving.

There are some who are insularly modern, who believe that the past is the bankrupt time, leaving no assets for us, but only a legacy of debts. They refuse to believe that the army that is marching forward can be fed from the rear. It is well to remind them that the great ages of renaissance in history were those when men sudddenly discovered the seeds of thought in the granary of the past.

The unfortunate people, who have lost the harvest of their past, have lost their present age. They have missed their seeds for cultivation, and go a-begging for their bare livelihood. We must not imagine that we are one of these disinherited peoples of the world. The time has come for us to break open the treasure trove of our ancestors and use it for our commerce of life. Let us, with its help, make our future our own—never continue our existence as the eternal rag-picker at other people's dustbins.

XVI

So far I have dwelt only upon the intellectual aspect of education, because with this we are familiar, because, like the moon, we, in modern India, present to the sun of the World-culture only one side of our life, which is the intellectual side; we do not yet fully realize that our other sides also require the same light for their illumination. From the educational point of view we know Europe where it is scientific, or at best literary. So our notion of modern culture is limited within the boundary lines of grammar and the laboratory. We almost completely ignore the æsthetic life of man, leaving it uncultivated, allowing weeds to grow there.

Therefore again I have to give utterance to a truism and say with profound seriousness that music and the fine arts are among the highest means of national self-expression, without which the people remain inarticulate.

Our conscious mind occupies only a superficial layer of our life; the sub-conscious mind is almost fathomless in its depth—where the wisdom of countless ages grows up from its base, like the great continents, beyond our ken. Our conscious mind finds its expression in numerous deliberate activities which pass and repass before our view. Our sub-conscious mind, where dwells our soul, must also have its adequate media of expression. These media are poetry and music and the arts; herein the complete personality of man finds its utterance.

Our newspapers are prolific, our meeting places are vociferous; in these we wear out to shreds the things we have borrowed from our English teachers, and make the air dismal and damp with the tears of our grievances. But where are our arts, which, like the outbreak of spring flowers, are the spontaneous overflow of our deeper nature, of our spiritual abundance of wealth? Must we be condemned to carry to the end the dead load of dolorous dumbness? Must we, like miserable outcasts, be deprived of our place in the festival of national culture, and wait at the outer court, where colour is not for us, nor the forms of delight, nor the songs? Must ours be the education of a prison-house, with hard labour and with a drab dress cut to the limits of minimum decency and necessity? Do we not know that the perfection of colour and form and expression belongs to the perfection of vitality—that the joy of life is only the other side of the strength of life?

The timber merchant may think that the flowers and foliage are mere frivolous decorations of a tree, but he will know to his cost that if these are suppressed, the timber also follows them.

During the Moghal period, music and art in India found a great impetus from the rulers, because their whole life was in this land, not merely their official life; and it is the wholeness of a man from which originates Art. Our English teachers are birds of passage; they cackle to us, but do not sing—their true heart is not in this land of their exile. The natural place of their art and music is in Europe, where they are so deep in the soil that they cannot be transferred to a distant land, unless the soil itself is removed.

We see the European, where he is learned, where he is masterful, where he is busily constructive in his trade and politics, but not where he is artistically creative. That is the reason why modern Europe has not been revealed to us in her complete personality, but only in her intellectual power and utilitarian activities; and therefore she has only touched our intellect and evoked our utilitarian ambitions.

The mutilation of life owing to this narrowness of

culture must no longer be encouraged. In the proposed centre of our cultures, music and art must have their prominent seats of honour, and not merely a tolerant nod of recognition. The different systems of music and different schools of art, which lie scattered in the different ages and provinces of India, and in the different strata of society, have to be brought together there and studied.

Thus a real standard of æsthetic taste will be formed, by the help of which our own art-expression will grow in strength and riches, enabling us to judge all foreign arts with the soberness of truth and to appropriate from them ideas and forms without incurring the charge of plagiarism.

XVII

All the time that I have been developing my ideas in this paper a secret uneasiness has never been absent from my mind, reminding me that these ideas would have to be submitted to the scrutiny of practical men—those men who have a natural suspicion of all pictures of completeness because of their perfection. They are sure to ask with pitiless gravity: "All that you discuss and describe may be true, or what is far worse, beautiful—but is it possible?"

Not being a practical man myself, my answer will be: "Whatever is true is real. Reality is related to truth, as the canvas to the picture—it must be there at the back." And if my ideal of the centre of Indian culture has any truth, it can be, and therefore must be, realized at all costs.

The one practical question which has to be answered, before all else, is the economic question: what adjustments should be made whereby such institutions can naturally maintain themselves and one day be independent, not only of the patronage of the rich, but of the dead imposition of their own accumulated funds. The wealth and honour which, once for all, are bequeathed to us, which we do not have to earn or produce, which never cease to be, whether we deserve them or not—these gradually and inevitably cripple our life and are sure to make us indolent and exclusive, bringing about stagnation of soul. They remain like the marble landing-stairs of a river, when the stream has changed its course. Therefore we must think out some scheme by which our truly national organization should be made to earn its own necessities by its own constant efforts, and thus perpetually keep in real touch with the life of the future ages and not continue its existence as a parasite feeding upon the charity of the past.

We are thus faced with two stupendous problems: the first, about our poverty of intellectual life, the second, about the poverty of our material life.

The first, I have discussed in some detail in this paper. I have come to the conclusion that for the perfection of our mental life the co-ordination of all our cultural resources is necessary. I have found that our present English education is, for our minds, a kind of food which contains only one particular ingredient needful for our vitality, and even that not fresh, but dried and packed in tins. In our true food we must have co-ordination of all different ingredients—and most of these, not as laboratory products, or in a desiccated condition, but as organic things, similar to our own living tissues.

Our material poverty, likewise, can only be removed by the co-ordination of our material resources through the co-operation of our individual powers. And the basis of our institution should be laid upon this economic co-operation. It must not only instruct, but live; not only think, but produce. Our *tapovanas*, which were our natural Universities, were not abstracted from life. There the masters and students lived their full life; they gathered their fruit and fuel; they took their cattle to graze; and the spiritual education, which the students had, was a part of the spiritual life itself which comprehended all life. Our centre of culture should not only be the centre of the intellectual life of India, but the centre of her economic life also. It must cultivate land, breed cattle, to feed itself and its students; it must produce all necessaries, devising the best means and using the best materials, calling science to its aid. Its very existence should depend upon the success of its industrial ventures carried out on the co-operative principle, which will unite the teachers and students in a living and active bond of necessity. This will give us also a practical industrial training, whose motive force is not the greed of profit.

Such an institution must group round it all the neighbouring villages and vitally unite them with itself in all its economic endeavours. Their housing accommodation, sanitation, the improvement of their moral and intellectual life—these should form the object of the social side of its activity. In a word, it should never be like a meteor—only a stray fragment of a world—but a complete world in itself, self-sustaining, independent, rich with ever-renewing life, radiating light across space and time, attracting and maintaining round it a planetary system of dependent bodies, imparting life-breath to the complete man, who is intellectual as well as economic, bound by social bonds and aspiring towards spiritual freedom.

XVIII

Before I conclude my paper, a delicate question remains to be considered: what must be the religious teaching that is to be given in our centre of Indian culture, which I may name *Visva-Bharati*? The question has been generally shirked in the case of the schools which we call national. A National University, in our minds, has been only another name for a Hindu University. So, whenever we give any thought to the question, we think of the Hindu religion alone. Unable as we are to rise to the conception of the Great India, we try to divide it, in the case of our culture, just as we have done by our religious rites and social customs. In other words, the idea of such unity as we are capable of achieving for ourselves not only fails to rouse enthusiasm in our hearts, but gives rise to some amount of antipathy.

Be that as it may, it has to be admitted that the world is full of different religious sects and will probably always remain so. It is no use lamenting over, or quarrelling with, this fact. There is a private corner for me in my house with a little table, which has its special fittings of pen and ink-stand and paper, and here I can best do my writing and other work. There is no reason to run down, or run away from, this corner of mine, because in it I cannot invite and provide seats for all my friends and guests. It may be that this corner is too narrow, or too close, or too untidy, so that my doctor may object, my friends remonstrate, my enemies sneer; but all that has nothing to do with the present case. My point is that if all the rooms in my house be likewise solely for my own special convenience; if there be no reception room for my friends, or accommodation for my guests, then indeed am I blameworthy. Then with bowed head must I confess that in my house no great meeting of friends can ever take place.

Religious sects are formed in every country and every age owing to a diversity of historical causes. There will always be many, who, by tradition and temperament, find special solace in belonging to a particular sect; and also there will be others who think that the finding of such solace can only be allowed as legitimate within the pale of their own. Between such, there needs must be quarrels. Making ample provision for such inevitable and interminable squabbles, can there be no wide meeting place, where all sects may gather together and forget their differences? Has India, in her religious ideals, no such space for the common light of day and open air for all humanity? The vigour with which the sectarian fanatic will shake his head, makes one doubt it; the bloodshed which so frequently occurs for such trivial causes, makes one doubt it; the cruel and insulting distinctions between man and man which are kept alive under the sanction of religion, make one doubt it. Still, in spite of all these, when I turn to look back to India's own pure culture—in those ages when it flourished in its truth—I am emboldened to assert that it is there. Our forefathers did spread a single pure white carpet whereon all the world was cordially invited to take its seat in amity and good fellowship. No quarrel could have arisen there; for He, in whose name the invitation went forth, for all time to come, was Santam, Sivam, Advaitam—the Peaceful, in the heart of all conflicts; the Good, who is revealed through all losses and sufferings; the One, in all diversities of creation. And in His name was this eternal truth declared in ancient India:

आत्मवत् सर्वभूतेषु यः पश्यति स पश्यति ।

He alone sees, who sees all beings as himself.